Metaphysical Healing

By
JOEL S. GOLDSMITH

Martino Publishing
Mansfield Centre, CT
2011

Martino Publishing
P.O. Box 373,
Mansfield Centre, CT 06250 USA

www.martinopublishing.com

ISBN   978-1-61427-101-7

© 2011 Martino Publishing

All rights reserved. No new contribution to this publication may be reproduced, stored in a retrieval system, or transmitted, in any form or by any means, electronic, mechanical, photocopying, recording, or otherwise, without the prior permission of the Publisher.

Cover design by T. Matarazzo

Printed in the United States of America On 100% Acid-Free Paper

Metaphysical Healing

By
JOEL S. GOLDSMITH

WILLING PUBLISHING COMPANY
3524 NORTH BROADWAY AVENUE
LOS ANGELES 31 • CALIFORNIA

Copyright, 1947
by Joel S. Goldsmith

Printed in the United States of America by
Willing Publishing Co.
Los Angeles 31, California

"Unless the Lord build the house, they labor in vain that build it."

Psalm 127

Illumination dissolves all material ties and binds men together with the golden chains of spiritual understanding; it acknowledges only the leadership of the Christ; it has no ritual or rule but the divine, impersonal universal Love; no other worship than the inner Flame that is ever lit at the shrine of Spirit. This union is the free state of spiritual brotherhood. The only restraint is the discipline of Soul, therefore we know liberty without license; we are a united universe without physical limits; a divine service to God without ceremony or creed. The illumined walk without fear—by Grace.

(From the book, *"The Infinite Way.)*

METAPHYSICAL HEALING

Healings are always in proportion to our understanding of the truth about God, man, idea, body. Healing has nothing to do with someone "out there" called a patient. When anyone asks for spiritual help or healing, that ends their part in what follows until they acknowledge their so-called healing. We are not concerned with the so-called patient, the claim, the cause of the illness or its nature, nor with his sins or fears. We are now concerned only with the truth of being — the truth of God, man, idea, body. The activity of this truth in our consciousness is the Christ, Saviour or healing influence.

Failure to heal is the result of much mis-knowledge of the truth of God, man, idea, body, and this mis-knowledge stems primarily from orthodox religious beliefs which have not been rooted out of our thought.

Few realize to what extent they are blinded by superstitious orthodoxy.

There is only one answer to the question, What is God? and that answer is I AM. God is the Mind, the Life of the individual. Any mental hedging or inner reservation on this subject will result in ultimate failure. There is but one universal I whether it is being spoken by Jesus Christ or John Smith. When Jesus revealed: "He that seeth me seeth him that sent me," he was revealing a universal Truth or Principle. There must be no quibbling about this. You either understand this truth or you do not — and if you do not there is no need for you to seek any further reason for failure to heal. The revelation of Jesus the Christ is clear. "I am the way, the truth, and the life." Unless you can accept this as a principle, therefore as the truth about you and about every individual, you have no foundation upon which to stand. The truth is that God is the Mind and Life of the individual. God is the only "I."

Next comes the question, What is man? and the answer is that man is idea, body, manifestation. My body is idea, or manifes-

"I will never be without my body" (as marked)

tation. Likewise my business, home, wealth, — these exist as idea or manifestation, expression, reflection. For this reason and for no other my body is the exact image and likeness of my consciousness and reflects or expresses the qualities, character and nature of my own consciousness of existence.

So far then we understand that "I" am God; that God is the Mind and Life of the individual; that my body exists as the idea of God. God, or I AM, is universal, infinite, omnipotent and omnipresent; therefore, the idea body is equally indestructible, imperishable, eternal. It was never born and will never die. I shall never be without the conscious awareness of my body; therefore, I shall never be without my body.

When we look out upon the world with our eyes we are not beholding our bodies, we are not seeing this infinite divine idea body, we are beholding a more or less universal *concept* of the idea. As we see a healthy body, a beautiful flower or tree, we are seeing a good concept of the idea body, flower, tree. When we see an aging, ailing body or withered flower or decaying tree, we

CONCEPTS

are beholding an erroneous concept of the divine idea. As we improve our concepts of idea, body, manifestation, we term this improving of concepts, *healing*. Actually nothing has happened to the so-called patient or his body — the change has come in the individual's consciousness and becomes visible as improved belief or healing. For this reason the healer alone must accept responsibility for healing and never try to shift the blame for non-healing onto the person who asked for help. *That individual* is I AM, Life, Truth and Love, and his body exists as perfect spiritual eternal harmonious idea subject only to the laws of Principle, Mind, Soul, Spirit — and it is our privilege, duty and responsibility to know this truth and the truth will make free every person who turns to us.

As individual, infinite spiritual consciousness, I embody my universe, I embody or include the idea body, home, activity, income, health, wealth, companionship, and these are subject only to spiritual law and life. The body is not self-acting, it is governed harmoniously by spiritual power. When the body appears to be discordant, inactive, overactive, changing, paining, it is always the belief that the body is self-acting; that it of itself has the power to move or not move, to ache, pain, sicken or die. This is not true. The body is not self-acting. It has no intelligence or activity of its own. All action is Mind action, therefore omnipotent good action. When we know this truth, the body responds to this knowing or understanding of Truth. No change then takes place in the body because the error never was there. It is entirely exchanging a concept for the truth that already is, always has been and ever will be. Remember there is no patient "out there" and no body out there to be healed, improved or corrected. Always it is a false concept or belief to be corrected in individual thought.

When we begin to understand that the body is not self-acting; that it responds only to the stimulus of Mind, we can disregard so-called inharmonious bodily conditions and abide in the truth that Life is forever expressing itself harmoniously, perfectly and eternally as the divine idea, body.

The understanding that I AM—individual infinite spiritual consciousness embodying every right idea and governing them harmoniously — brings forth health, harmony, home, employment, recognition, peace, joy and dominion. The understanding that this is true of every individual dispels the illusion of hate, enmity, opposition, etc. This also makes of you a practitioner, a healer, a teacher, whether or not professionally engaged in the work.

We come now to face our orthodox superstitions and to leave them. Was Jesus sent into the world by God to save it from sin, disease, or slavery? No. God, the infinite Principle, Life, Truth and Love, knows no error, no evil, no sin and no sinner. Jesus so clearly apprehended this truth that this apprehension became the Saviour, Healer, Teacher even as it will in you. *The activity of Truth in individual consciousness is the only Christ.* No person is ever the Christ. The activity of Truth in individual consciousness constitutes the only Christ, the ever-present Christ who was "before Abraham." The activity of Truth in your consciousness is the Christ of you. The activity of Truth in the consciousness of Buddha revealed the nature of sin, disease and death to be illusion or mirage. The activity of Truth in the consciousness of Jesus Christ revealed the nothingness of matter; it unfolded as a Healing Consciousness before which sin and disease disappeared and death was overcome. Every erroneous concept, whether of body or business, health or church, must disappear as the right idea of these appear in individual and collective consciousness.

What about immaculate conception or spiritual birth? The immaculate conception or spiritual birth is the dawning in individual consciousness of the activity of Truth or Christ idea. It appeared in Jesus as the revelation that "I am the way, the truth, and the life" "I am the resurrection and the life"—"He that seeth me, seeth him that sent me." The activity of Truth in my consciousness, the Christ of me, is revealing that I am individual, infinite, spiritual consciousness embodying my universe, including my body, my health, wealth, practice, income, home, companionship, eternality and immortality.

Let the activity of Truth in your consciousness be your first and last and only concern, and the Christ of you will also reveal itself in an individual, infinite Way.

There is no evil. Let us therefore stop the resistance to the particular discord or inharmony of human existence which now confronts us. These apparent discords will disappear as we are able to cease our resistance to them. We are able to do this only in proportion to our realization of the spiritual nature of the universe. Since this is true, it is evident that neither heaven nor earth can contain error of any nature and therefore the unillumined human thought is seeing error in the very place where God shines through; discord where harmony is; hate where love abounds; fear where confidence really is.

The work on which we have embarked is the realization that we are individual infinite spiritual consciousness embodying within ourselves all good. This is the song we will sing, the sermon we will preach,

NIAGARA

the lesson we will teach, and until realization comes, this is our theme, our motif. It is the silver cord of Truth running through every message.

Nothing can come to you; nothing can be added. You are already that place in consciousness through which infinity is pouring. That which we term your humanhood must be still so as to be a clear transparency through which your infinite individual Self may appear, express or reveal itself.

When we view Niagara Falls from the front, we might assume that it could run dry with so much water continually pouring over the Falls. Looking behind the immediate scene, we behold Lake Erie, and realize that actually there is no Niagara, that this is but a name given to Lake Erie at a point where Erie pours over the Falls. The infinity of Niagara Falls is assured by virtue of the fact that actually the source of Niagara, that which constitutes Niagara, is really Lake Erie.

So with us. We are that place where God becomes visible. We are the Word made flesh. Our source, and that which con-

I LOVE THIS

stitutes us, is God—infinite divine Being. We are God-being, God-appearing, God-manifesting. That is the true glory of our being.

The story is told of Marconi, that when he was very young, he told friends that he would be the one to give wireless to the world and not the many older seekers who had been experimenting for years. After he fulfilled his promise he was asked why he had been so certain that he would succeed. His answer was that the other scientists were seeking first to discover a means to overcome resistance in the air to the messages that would be sent through the air, whereas he had already discovered there was no resistance.

The world is fighting a power of evil; we have discovered there is no such power. While materia medica seeks to overcome or cure disease and theology struggles to overcome sin, we have learned there is no reality to disease or sin and our so-called healings are brought about through this understanding.

We know that there are these human

appearances called sin and disease, but we know that because of the infinite spiritual nature of our being, they are not realities of being; they are not evil power; they have no Principle to support them; therefore, they exist only as unrealities accepted as realities, illusion accepted as condition, the misinterpretation of what actually is.

We bind ourselves by believing there is power outside of us—power for good or for evil. All power is given to *you*. And this power is always good because of the infinite source whence it flows. The recognition of this great fact brings a peace and a joy untold, yet felt by all who come within range of your thought. It makes you beloved of men. It brings you recognition and reward. It establishes you in the thoughts of men and becomes the foundation of an eternal good will.

Whenever you are faced with a problem, regardless of its nature, seek the solution within your own consciousness. Instead of running around here and there; instead of seeking an answer from this or that person; instead of looking for the solution outside

> Try again if a first you don't succeed.

of yourself, turn within. In the quiet and calm of your own mind, let the answer to your problem unfold itself. If, the first or second or third time you turn in peace to the kingdom within, you fail to perceive the completed picture, try again. You will not be too late, nor will the solution appear too late. As you learn to depend on this means for the working out of your problems and experiences, you will become more and more adept in quickly discerning your mind's revelation of harmony. Too long have we sought our health, peace and prosperity outside ourselves. Now let us go within and learn that there is never a failure nor a disappointment in the whole realm of our consciousness. Nor will we ever find delays or betrayals when we find the calm of our own Soul and the presence of an infinite Principle governing, guarding, guiding and protecting every step of our journey through life.

Do not be surprised now when the outstanding truth unfolds to you that your consciousness is the all-power and the only power acting upon your affairs, controlling

Consciousness is The Only Power.

and maintaining your health, revealing to you the intelligence and direction necessary for your success in any and every walk of life. Does this astonish you? No wonder! Heretofore you have believed that somewhere there existed a deific power, a supreme presence, which, *if you could reach,* might aid you or even heal your body of its ills. Now it becomes clear to you that the universal Mind or Consciousness is the mind of the individual man and *it* is the all-power and ever-presence which can never leave you nor forsake you, and it is "closer than breathing." And you need not pray to it, petition it or in any way seek its favor,—you need but this recognition leading to the complete realization of this truth. From now on you will relax and *feel* the constant assurance of the presence and power of this illumined consciousness. You can now say, "I will not fear what man shall do unto me." No more will you fear conditions or circumstances seemingly outside of you or beyond your control. Now you know that all that can transpire in your experience is occurring within your consciousness and therefore subject to its government and control.

Nor will you ever forget the depth of feeling accompanying this revelation within you, nor the sense of confidence and courage that immediately follows it. Life is no longer a problem-filled series of events, but a joyous succession of unfolding delights. Failure is recognized as the result of a universal belief in a power outside of ourselves. Success is the natural consequence of our realization of infinite power within.

Release from fear, worry and doubt leaves us free to function normally, healthfully and confidently. The body acts immediately from the stimulus coming to it from within. New vitality, strength and bodily peace follow us naturally as rest follows sleep. Little do we know of the depth of the riches within us until we come to know the realm of our own consciousness, the kingdom of our mind.

When we become still and go into the temple of our being for the answer to some important question, or the solution of a vital problem, it is well that we do not

formulate some idea of our own, or outline a plan, or let our wish in the matter father our thought. Rather should we still the thinking mind so far as possible and adopt a listening attitude. It is not the personal sense of mind (or conscious mind) which is to supply the answer. Nor is it the educated mind or the mind formed of our environment and experience, but the universal Mind, the Reality of us, the creative Consciousness. And this is best heard when the senses and reasoning mind are silent.

This inner Mind not only shows us the solution to any problem and the right direction to take in any situation, but, being the universal Mind, it is the consciousness of every individual and brings every person and circumstance together for the good of the whole.

Obviously we cannot look to this universal Consciousness to work with us for anyone's destruction or loss. What is accomplished in and through the kingdom of our mind is always constructive individually and collectively. It can therefore never be the means of harm, loss or injury to another.

My mind's activity is one with other minds. Who can help in a particular situation. No unsolved problems

Nor do we direct our thought at another, or project it outside ourselves in any direction. That which our mind is unfolding to us, is at the time operating as the consciousness of all concerned. We need never concern ourselves with "reaching" some other mind, or influencing some other person. Remember that the activity of Mind unfolding as us, is the influence unto all who can possibly be affected by or concerned in the problem or situation. There are no unsolved problems in Mind and this same Mind which is our own consciousness is the only power necessary to establishing and maintaining the harmony of all that concerns us. It is our turning within that brings forth the answer already established. Our listening attitude makes us receptive to the presence and the power within us. Our periods of silent contemplation reveal the infinite force and constructive energy and intelligent direction always abiding in us. Thus we discover in our mental realm the Aladdin's Lamp. Instead of rubbing and wishing, we turn in silence and listen—and all that is necessary for the harmony and success of life flows forth abundantly and we learn to live joyously, healthfully, and successfully—not by reason of any person or circumstance outside ourselves, but because of the influence and grace within our own being.

No longer is it necessary to try to dominate our business associates or members of our family. The law within us maintains our rights and privileges. Every right desire of our heart is fulfilled now and without struggle or strife, without fear or doubt. The more we learn to relax and quickly contemplate our real desires, the more quickly and more easily are they achieved. It is not required of us that we suffer our way through life or strive endlessly for some desired good—but we have failed to perceive the presence of an inner law capable of establishing and maintaining our outer welfare.

It seems strange to us at first to realize that inner laws govern outer events—and it may at first appear difficult to achieve the state of consciousness wherein these laws of our inner being come into tangible expression. We will achieve it, however, in proportion to our ability to relax mentally; to gain an inner calm and peace; and therein quietly contemplate the revelations which come to us from within. Quietness and confidence soon bring us face to face with Reality, the real laws governing us.

Lest the question should arise in your thought as to how a law operating in your consciousness (and without conscious effort or direction) can affect individuals and circumstances outside yourself, let me ask you to watch the result of your recognition of the inner laws and learn this through observation.

We are yet to become aware of the fact that we embrace our world within ourselves; that all that exists of persons, places and things lives only within our own consciousness. We could never become aware of anything outside the realm of our own mind. And all that is within our mental kingdom is joyously and harmoniously directed and sustained by the laws within. We do not direct or enforce these laws; they eternally operate within us and govern the world without.

The peace within becomes the harmony without. As our thought takes on the nature of the inner freedom, it loses its sense of fear, doubt, or discouragement. As the realization of our dominion dawns in thought, more assurance, confidence and certainty become evident. We become a new being, and the world reflects back to us our own higher attitude toward it. Gradually an understanding of our fellow man and his problems unfolds to us from within, and more love flows out from us, more tolerance, co-operativeness, helpfulness, and compassion, and we find the world responds to our newer concept of it, and then all the universe rushes to us to pour its riches and treasures in our lap.

Many fine treaties and covenants have been signed by nations and men, and nearly all have failed, because no document is any better than the character of those who administer it. When we become imbued with the fire of our inner being, we no longer need contracts and agreements in writing because it becomes first nature with us to be just, honest, intelligent and kind—and these qualities are met in all those who become part of our experience in the home, office, shop, and in all our walks of life. The good revealed in our consciousness returns to us, "pressed down, shaken together, and running over."

In this new consciousness we are less angered by the acts of other people; less impatient with their short-comings; less disturbed by their failings. And likewise, instead of being hampered and restricted by external conditions, we either do not meet with them or else brush right by them with but little concern. We realize that something within us is ruling our universe; an inner presence is maintaining outer harmony. The peace and quiet of our own Soul is the law of harmony and success to our world of daily experience.

All that has gone before this is as nothing unless you have seen that over and above all "knowing the truth," you must be overshadowed by the Christ.

When the Christ dawns in individual consciousness, the sense of personal self diminishes. This Christ becomes our real being.

We have no desires, no will, no power of our own. The Christ overshadows our personal selfhood. We still perceive in the background this finite sense and at times it tries to assert itself and even dominate the scene. "For the good that I would I do not: but the evil which I would not, that I do," says Paul.

But let it be clear to you that the personal self cannot heal, teach or govern harmoniously. It must be held in abeyance that the Christ may have full dominion within our consciousness.

The work that is done with the letter of Truth, with declarations and so-called treatments, is insignificant compared with what is accomplished when we have surrendered our will and action to the Christ.

Christ comes to our consciousness most clearly in those moments when we come face to face with problems for which we have no answer, and no power to surmount, and we realize that "I can of mine own self do nothing." In these moments of self-effacement, the gentle Christ overshadows us, permeates our consciousness and brings the "Peace, be still," to the troubled mind.

In this Christ we find rest, peace, comfort and healing. The unlabored power of spiritual sense possesses us and discords and inharmonies fade away as darkness disappears with the coming of light. Indeed, it is comparable only to the breaking of dawn; and the gradual influx of divine Light colors the scenes in our mind and dispels one by one the illusions of sense, the darker places in human thought.

The stress of daily living would deprive us of this great Spirit unless we are careful to retire often into the sanctuary of our inner being and there let the Christ be our honored guest.

Never let vain conceit or a belief in personal power keep you from this sacred experience. Be willing. Be receptive. Be still.

OTHER BOOKS

By

JOEL S. GOLDSMITH

The Infinite Way $2.00
Meditation and Prayer . . . . . $.25
Metaphysical Healing . . . . . $.25
Business and Salesmanship . . . . $.25
Supply : . . . . $.25

Order from

WILLING PUBLISHING COMPANY
3524 North Broadway Avenue
Los Angeles 31, California

Lightning Source UK Ltd.
Milton Keynes UK
UKOW03f2231170914

238771UK00001B/229/P